FLY-FISHING

by Tim Seeberg

Content Adviser: Matt Wilhelm, Aquatic/Angling Educator,
Federation of Fly Fishers, Bozeman, Montana

Published in the United States of America by The Child's World®
PO Box 326 • Chanhassen, MN 55317-0326 • 800-599-READ • www.childsworld.com

Acknowledgments

The Child's World®: Mary Berendes, Publishing Director

Editorial Directions, Inc.: E. Russell Primm, Editorial Director; Halley Gatenby, Line Editor;
Susan Hindman, Copyeditor; Elizabeth K. Martin and Katie Marsico, Assistant Editors;
Matthew Messbarger, Editorial Assistant; Peter Garnham, Christine Simms, and
Kathy Stevenson, Fact Checkers; Tim Griffin/IndexServ, Indexer; James Buckley Jr.,
Photo Researcher and Photo Selector

The Design Lab: Kathleen Petelinsek, Design and Art Production

Photos

Cover: Corbis
Peter Beck/Corbis: 19, 22; Corbis: 4, 26; MacDuff Everton/Corbis: 10; Natalie Forbes/
Corbis: 16; Raymond Gehman/Corbis: 14; Phil Kelley: 12 (2); Roy Morsch/Corbis: 25; Dale
Spartas/Corbis: 13, 24, 28, 29; Sports Gallery/Al Messerschmidt: 7, 9; Karl Weatherly/
Corbis: 15, 17; Bob Winsett/Corbis: 23.

Library of Congress Cataloging-in-Publication Data

Seeberg, Tim.
  Fly-fishing / by Tim Seeberg.
    p. cm. — (Kids' guides)
  Summary: An introduction to fly-fishing, describing basic techniques, safety
measures, the necessary equipment, and popular places to fish.
  ISBN 1-59296-034-0 (lib. bdg. : alk. paper)
  1. Fly fishing—Juvenile literature. [1. Fly fishing. 2. Fishing.] I. Title. II. Series.
  SH456.S44 2004
  799.12'4—dc22   2003017803

CONTENTS

WHAT IS FLY-FISHING?

HUNDREDS OF SMALL INSECTS DANCE

above and on the surface of the water. Off to the side, another one lands and rests, disturbing nothing and being moved only by the current and the breeze.

In fact, this one is not an insect. It is a small creation of feathers, hair, and thread tied together to look like an insect. The feathers and hair disguise the hook to which they are tied.

Lured by a tasty "fly," this fish is about to make a flyfisherman very happy!

The "insect" is actually tied to several feet of very thin, clear string. And you are in control, connected to the other end of that string, or line, by the fishing rod in your hand. Just as you planned, your imitation insect—called a fly—floats right above the shadow under the water that you suspect might be a fish.

Suddenly, the water around the fly splashes upward. It is a fish! In a split-second motion, the fish darts up from its holding spot, sunlight reflecting off its silvery side. It launches itself out of the water and then, with a flip of its tail, dives back down.

At that moment, you feel a slight tug. The fish has taken your fly! Instinctively, you quickly raise the tip of your rod. You feel an even stronger pull. You've hooked it! And the fight is on.

This combination of grace and strength, **strategy** and luck, calm and excitement is what fly-fishing is all about. You might be in a boat on a clear lake, on the grassy bank of a pond, along a seacoast, or standing in a gentle stream or a rushing river. But the magic is the same.

Fly-fishing is easy and fun to learn. Everyone can do it. Learning with your family or friends makes it even better. In fact, someone you know is probably a fly-fisher. Ask around to find out. Like most great things in life, fly-fishing is much more fun when you share it with other people.

CHAPTER ONE

TACKLING TACKLE

FISHING EQUIPMENT OF ANY SORT IS

called tackle. You will use your tackle to get your fly to the fish and, when you catch a fish, to bring the fish to you. You do not need much tackle to begin fly-fishing—only five items: a fly, a fly rod, a fly **reel,** a fly line, and a **leader.**

Any experienced fly-fisher can advise you about the tackle that is right for you. Also, many fly-fishing shops and general sporting goods stores offer kits specifically made for beginners. If you cannot find one of these kits, you can probably still get all your tackle at one sporting goods store.

Be sure to tell the salesperson if you have ever been fly-fishing before. If you have done any other kind of fishing, tell the salesperson that, too. Also say where and when you will be fly-fishing and what type of fish you will be trying to catch.

In fly-fishing, the fly is the bait. Flies are made in many different sizes, shapes, and weights. Most are tied from some combination of feathers, animal hair, and thread, although many flies include other types of materials. The fly is tied to a hook. When a fish eats the fly and then tries to spit it back out, the hook catches in the fish's mouth.

Often, the fly is tied to look like an insect, a small fish, a leech, or just about anything else a fish might eat. Some flies are

not intended to look like anything natural. These flies are used to catch fish by getting the fish angry or excited so they attack it.

There are thousands of types of flies designed to catch dozens of types of fish. Many fly-fishers enjoy tying (making) their own flies. The four main types of flies are dry flies, wet flies, nymphs, and streamers.

Colorful "flies" are tied to look like real-life insects or fish.

Dry flies—Dry flies float high on the surface of the water. They are often designed to look like an insect that has just landed there. Some are imitations of a frog or a mouse that larger fish might like. Catching a fish with a dry fly is very exciting—you get to see it happen because the fish comes up to the fly.

Wet flies—Wet flies do not float on the surface of the water. Instead, they rest in or just below the surface of the water.

Nymphs—Many insects are born under water and live there as nymphs until they become adults. Some fish, especially trout, eat more nymphs than any other food. Nymph flies are designed to look like these very young insects. They drift and bounce along or near the bottom of the water.

Streamers—Streamer flies resemble the smaller fish that are eaten by larger fish. Streamers are intended to catch fish under the surface of the water. Streamers move when the fly-fisher **strips** the line by pulling in short sections of it. This makes the fly look like a swimming fish.

The fly line is a little thinner than a strand of spaghetti and is covered with a smooth, slick vinyl coating. Fly lines are available in several weights, types, and colors. Lighter-weight lines are used for **casting** smaller flies, and heavier-weight lines are used for larger, heavier flies. The weight of the line should match the rod being used. Usually the correct line weight is written on the rod, close to where you hold it.

There are different types of line. Some lines float near the surface, while others sink towards the bottom.

The reel is a round, spinning device that attaches to the

rod. The line is wound tightly and evenly around it. As you cast the line, the reel spins and releases it. Then, as you pull in the line, the reel gathers it. Your reel should match the type of rod and line you'll be using. You might also use different reels for different types of fish.

The fly is attached to the line with a leader so that the fly will land correctly on the water. The leader is made of very thin nylon that narrows at the end to a small **tippet.** Leader

The round device is the reel; it is attached near the bottom of the rod.

A fishing vest is a handy way to carry flyfishing gear.

size is determined by the size of the fish you want to catch. The length of the leader also depends on the fishing conditions. In a lake, longer leaders are used. On a windy day, a shorter leader is usually better. Tippet size is determined by the size of the fly. For instance, for smaller fish and flies, you'll use thinner leaders with smaller tippets.

With all this gear in hand, you're ready to head for the water. Let's see if you can fool a fish into thinking your fly is a tasty snack.

FLY-FISHING GEAR

You'll always need your basic tackle—flies, fly rod, fly line, reel, and leader. Here are some other things to consider taking along. Some of them help you stay safe, while others help in dealing with your tackle and the fish. Special fishing vests or tackle boxes can help you carry this gear.

- Camera
- Fishing license (may be required for fishing in some places)
- Small first-aid kit (include insect repellent)
- Needle-nose pliers (to remove hooks from the fish)
- Nail clippers (for cutting line)
- Net hat (a cap that has a **mesh** rear)
- Sunglasses
- Sunscreen
- Life vest
- Water bottle
- Towel

CHAPTER TWO

TYING AND CASTING

ONCE YOUR GEAR IS ASSEMBLED AND

you're in a good place to fish, your first step is to assemble the fly line. A nail knot (see illustration) attaches the leader to the end of the fly line. At the end of the leader, a clinch knot (see picture) connects the fly to the leader.

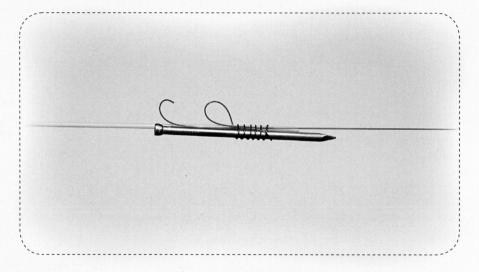

The nail knot (top, tied to a real nail to make it easier for you to see) and clinch knot are used to hold leader, line, and fly together.

Before casting, carefully tie the fly to the leader.

You need to pay close attention to tying the clinch knot correctly. This knot is closest to the fly. If it is sloppy or too big, the fish might see it and be scared away. Also, this knot has the most pressure on it when you catch a fish. If it is not tied correctly, it might break or come untied, and you would lose the fish (and your fly!). It's a good idea to prepare your line and leader connections before you leave to go fishing. A fly shop or an experienced **angler** can help you with this.

With your fly attached to your line, it is time to send it out onto or into the water to try to attract a fish. Casting, or fly-casting, is how you get your fly to the area of the water where you think a fish will take it. Fly-casting might look complicated

The backcast is the first step; lift your forearm to bring the rod tip back.

Whipping your arm lightly forward, try to float the fly out on the air before it lands on the water.

and difficult. Actually, it is simple, but it takes practice to get it right. If you are patient when you practice, casting will become as easy for you as throwing a ball. In fact, you will probably enjoy casting as much as any other part of fly-fishing.

Learning to fly-cast requires a lot of space around you. You don't need water to start practicing. The best place to learn and practice fly-casting is in a wide-open space with short grass. Here is a quick rundown of the key steps in casting.

First, set your fly rod on the ground. Walk to the tip of

your fly rod, pick up the end of your fly line, and walk 10 to 15 steps away from the rod. Set the line down so that it is straight, and walk back to your fly rod.

Then stand next to the handle of your fly rod with your feet pointing toward the tip of the rod. Your feet should be shoulder-width apart.

Now reach down and pick up your fly rod. Grip it with the hand you use for writing. Hold it as you would hold a flashlight, with your fingers wrapped underneath and your thumb on top. Don't make your grip too tight. The reel should be on the bottom, facing the ground.

The **back cast** is the way to start your cast. With your arm straight out in front of you, hold your rod so the tip is pointing at the end of your fly line in the grass. With one smooth and fast motion, lift your forearm until your hand is almost next to your head. Be sure to keep your elbow by your side—but not touching it—and do not bend your wrist. Let your arm and the rod continue to move backward slowly. When your hand is next to your ear, stop your arm and flick just your wrist backward. The fly line will straighten out in the air behind you. Let the fly line drop to the ground. You just completed a back cast!

The basic forward cast is the motion that places your fly where you want it to go. (This is the tricky part.) After you have completed your back cast, reverse the motion you just made. Smoothly and with force, move your hand forward, still keeping your elbow by your side. When your hand is just in front of your head, stop forcing the rod forward, snap your wrist forward,

As your cast ends, your arm is extended outward, pointing toward your target.

and let your arm and the rod continue to drift forward. As the fly line settles to the ground in front of you, keep your rod tip pointed at your fly.

Practice these motions separately until the fly line lands straight after both the back cast and the forward cast. Now you are ready to make a full cast. To make a full cast, start with a back cast, just as before. This time, just as the fly line straightens out in the air behind you, start your forward cast.

The best way to learn fly-casting is with the help of an experienced fly-fisher. Eventually, you will find that casting is like throwing. The more you do it, the better you will be.

A GOOD ANGLER . . .

- thinks, "Safety first!"
- gets out of the way when another angler has a fish on the line.
- does not enter the water near someone who is already there, unless invited.
- respects other people's property and obeys all property signs. If you pass through a gate, leave it as you found it (open or closed). If you want to fish on private property, ask the owner first.
- leaves the area cleaner than he or she found it. Never litter! Take all trash out with you.
- avoids making tracks whenever possible. If a trail already exists, use it.
- enters the water only when necessary. This helps protect the fish and the plants, animals, and insects the fish need.

CHAPTER THREE

FINDING FISH AND STAYING SAFE

YOU'VE GOT YOUR TACKLE AND OTHER

gear. You've practiced fly-casting. Now comes another key step:

finding the fish. Fish live nearly everywhere there is water with

enough food, oxygen, and **cover.** Look for creeks, streams,

rivers, ponds, or lakes near you that might hold fish.

A quiet stream
amid towering
pines is a great
place to fish.

Fish can often be found along the banks of a river or pond.

There are thousands of kinds of fish, but not all of them can live in the same kind of water. Different types of fish live in salt water (such as oceans), freshwater (most lakes, rivers, or streams), and brackish water. Brackish water is found where freshwater meets salt water, such as where rivers run into the sea.

Many fish need places to hide, such as aquatic plants, rocks, or logs. Cover protects them from enemies and puts them in position to catch an unsuspecting meal that is drifting or swimming by. That's why casting near cover can often be a good way to find a fish for your fly.

Just as fish need to be safe, safety should be important to you when you are fishing. Fly-fishing is not a dangerous sport, but you should prepare to stay safe and comfortable in the outdoors. It is possible to get caught unexpectedly in bad weather, to be bitten or stung by insects, to get too much sun, or even to get hooked yourself.

FLY-FISHING SAFETY

The best way to avoid danger or injuries when you go fly-fishing is to follow these important safety tips.

- **Beware of hooks.** They are very sharp. Barbless hooks are the best, but barbs on hooks can be pinched down for safety. Be careful when tying your fly to the leader. Do not cast when other people are close by. Always wear protective eyewear. Use pliers to remove a hook from a fish.

- **Know where you are.** Be aware of the potential hazards around you. Watch where you step because boulders, logs, and holes can cause you to slip and fall. Be careful fishing from boats: Try not to make sudden movements that will rock the boat. If you fish from a bridge, make sure fishing is allowed there, and watch out for cars, bikes, and people moving behind you.

- **Watch the weather.** Beware of lightning and other bad weather. Avoid sunburn by wearing proper clothing, including a hat that shades your face, ears, and neck. Be sure to wear sunscreen. You are at greater risk of sunburn when fishing because the sun's rays become stronger as they reflect off the water.

- **Protect your eyes.** Wear **polarized sunglasses** to protect your eyes. Polarized lenses also help you see through reflections on the surface of the water to spot fish more easily.

- **Avoid hypothermia.** Hypothermia is when your body temperature is dangerously low. Even on the hottest days, you can get too cold because of the low temperature of the water around you. Stay warm and dry as much as possible. If you get too wet and start shivering, dry off right away.

- **Know how to swim.** It is always important to keep a **personal flotation device** handy, even if you do know how to swim.

- **Fish with a friend.** Fishing with someone else is not only safer, it can also be more fun!

A scenic lake surrounded by snow-covered mountains makes an ideal fishing spot.

You've got your gear, you've found your fishing spot, and you're ready to fish safely. Now, let's catch a fish!

CHAPTER FOUR

CATCHING A FISH

WHERE DO YOU THINK A FISH MIGHT BE?

A few minutes of quiet observation can really pay off. You may see insects emerging, laying eggs, or dying on the surface of the water. You may see grasshoppers or ants floating or drifting. You might also see a fish rise from its cover to catch an insect. Observing will help you match your flies to the natural insects of the fishing spot.

Be careful when standing in moving water.

Carefully position yourself so you are close enough to be able to reach the area with your cast. Move cautiously so you don't scare the fish away. Using your casting technique, cast your fly to the place where you think the fish might be. As soon as you finish your cast, use your index finger to pinch the line coming off the reel against the rod. Do this with the hand that is holding the rod. When you hook a fish, this will prevent the fish from running away with the line. Remember that you will

Wearing water-proof boots and waders, you can easily move to the middle of shallow streams.

This is it! The fish is about to strike the fly . . . get ready for a fight!

probably have to cast many times and into many different areas before you catch a fish. Be patient.

When you see a fish take, or **strike,** your fly, or when you feel a tug on your line, quickly raise the tip of your rod to **set** the hook in the fish's mouth. Keep the rod tip high and the fly line tight. If the hook sets properly, the fish will be hooked. Immediately check to make sure you are standing in a safe place and are not in danger of losing your balance. If the fish pulls

A net can be a helpful addition to your fishing gear.

hard away from you, slightly loosen your pinch on the line and let the fish **run.** When you feel the fish stop pulling, quickly pull in as much line as you can with your non-casting hand.

Continue this give and take until the fish is no longer fighting hard to get away. You should **play** the fish as quickly as possible so as not to exhaust the fish. This will increase the fish's chance of survival if you decide to release it.

Again using your non-casting hand, pull in line until you have brought the fish within your reach. Try to keep it in the water. If you are with a person who has a net, let him or her scoop the fish into the net.

Proper handling of the fish is very important. If you are going to release the fish, keep it in the water as much as you can. Handle the fish as little as possible. Fish have a slippery film on their bodies called a slime coat. It helps protect them from disease, infection, and parasites. Wet your hand, then cradle the fish in your hand and hold on firmly, but do not squeeze too hard. Pinch the hook with your pliers and unhook the fish as gently as possible. This is easiest with barbless hooks.

Now hold the fish in the water. If it tries to swim away immediately, let it go. If it does not, it has not yet recovered from its struggle against your line. Move it gently forward and backward to get water and oxygen moving through its gills. This helps to revive it. Slowly loosen your hold, and the fish will swim off. When you do this for the first time, you will have practiced catch and release.

Fly-fishing is a terrific way to spend time by yourself or with family and friends. It can take a long time to master the skills, but once you do, you'll have a hobby for life. You'll learn more about nature, and sometimes you might even bring home dinner!

A successful flyfisherman displays a prize catch.

CATCH AND RELEASE

Catch and release is the practice of putting fish safely back into the water after you catch them. It was started in the 1930s and is very popular among fly-fishers and other types of anglers. In some places, regulations require you to release every fish you catch. Pay attention to the regulations in the area where you will be fishing.

Catch and release helps to protect the fish population and the aquatic **ecosystem.** It also helps to ensure there will always be enough fish for you to catch the next time out.

If you plan to keep the fish you catch, keep only what you plan to eat. Release all the others safely.

GLOSSARY

angler—a person who fishes with a hook, or an "angle"

back cast—casting a fly line in the direction opposite to the direction you want to place the fly

casting—using a fly rod to send a fly onto the water to attract a fish

cover—places fish hide

ecosystem—the connected environment (land, water, wildlife, plants) of a given area

leader—a small piece of equipment that attaches at one end to the fly line and at the other end to the fly

mesh—a type of material that is woven or knitted; it usually has an open texture with small and evenly spaced holes

personal flotation device—a suit or vest that will keep you afloat in the water; it is often referred to as a lifejacket

play—to struggle with the fish until you can pull it in

polarized sunglasses—sunglasses with special lenses that block glare

reel—a round, spinning device that attaches to the rod and holds line wound tightly and evenly around it

run—describes a fish pulling out a line as it tries to escape

set—to apply an upward motion of the fly rod or a quick tension on the fly line to make sure the hook penetrates the fish's mouth

strategy—a plan of action or way of doing things

strike—(1) the action of a fish trying to eat a fly; (2) the movement of the rod a fly angler makes to set the hook

strips—the action of pulling in short sections of the fly line to imitate a live insect or fish

tippet—the thin end of the leader; the part to which the fly is tied

FIND OUT MORE

For more information about fishing, visit your local tackle, fly-fishing or sporting goods store, contact your local fish and wildlife office, and check out the books and the Web site listed here.

Books

Campbell, Hugh. *Lightning's Tale: The Story of a Wild Trout.* Portland, Ore.: Frank Amato Publications, Inc., 2000.

Lucas, Kimberly H. (photographer). *Fly-Fishing with Trout-Tail: A Child's Journey.* Grosse Point Park, Mich.: Trout-Tail, LLC, 2003.

On the Web

Visit our home page for lots of links about fly-fishing:
http://www.childsworld.com/links.html

NOTE TO PARENTS, TEACHERS, AND LIBRARIANS: We routinely check our Web links to make sure they're safe, active sites—so encourage your readers to check them out!

INDEX

About the Author

Tim Seeberg is a writer based in Bend, Oregon. He has a lifelong love of the outdoors and is an avid fly fisherman. A graduate of UCLA, Tim has worked in advertising and public relations, and has also written about sports history.